I0796622

A Day in the Life of a Raccoon

Julie Murray

Abdo Kids Junior
is an Imprint of Abdo Kids
abdobooks.com

abdobooks.com

Published by Abdo Kids, a division of ABDO, P.O. Box 398166, Minneapolis, Minnesota 55439.

Printed in the United States of America, North Mankato, Minnesota.

102025

012026

Photo Credits: AdobeStock, Getty Images, Shutterstock

Production Contributors: Teddy Borth, Jennie Forsberg, Grace Hansen

Design Contributors: Candice Keimig, Pakou Moua

Library of Congress Control Number: 2025936499

Publisher's Cataloging-in-Publication Data

Names: Murray, Julie, author.

Title: A day in the life of a raccoon / by Julie Murray

Description: Minneapolis, Minnesota : Abdo Kids, 2026 | Series: A day in the life of an animal | Includes online resources and index.

Identifiers: ISBN 9798384907312 (lib. bdg.) | ISBN 9798384908012 (ebook) | ISBN 9798384908364 (read-to-me ebook)

Subjects: LCSH: Raccoon--Juvenile literature. | Raccoon--Behavior--Juvenile literature. | Nocturnal animals--Juvenile literature. | Nocturnal animals--Behavior--Juvenile literature. | Animal behavior—Juvenile literature. | Zoology--Juvenile literature.

Classification: DDC 599.7632--dc23

Table of Contents

A Raccoon's Day

The sun is setting.
The raccoon's day
is just beginning.

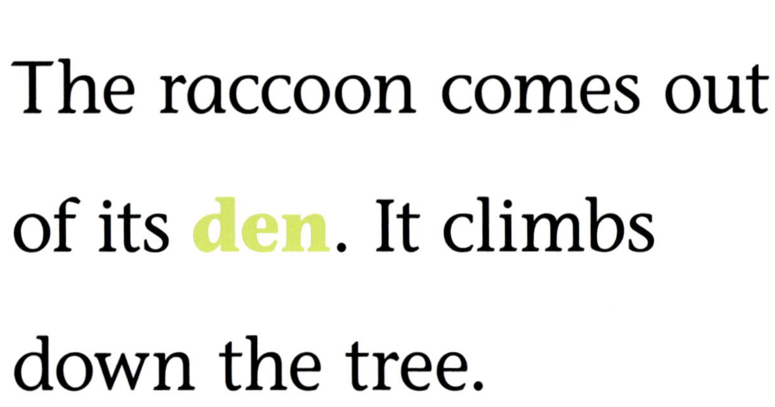

The raccoon comes out of its **den**. It climbs down the tree.

It searches for food.

It finds some acorns.

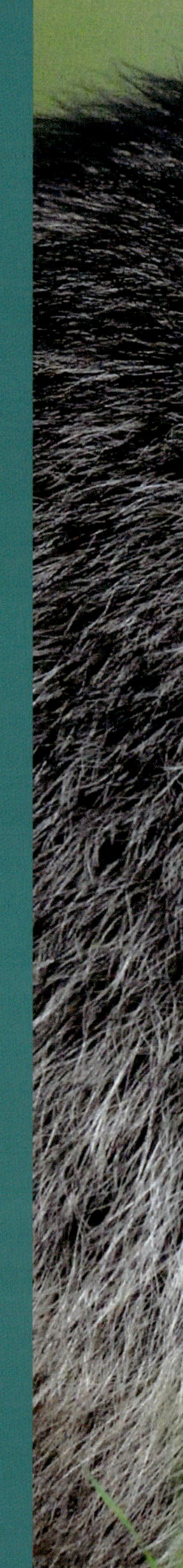

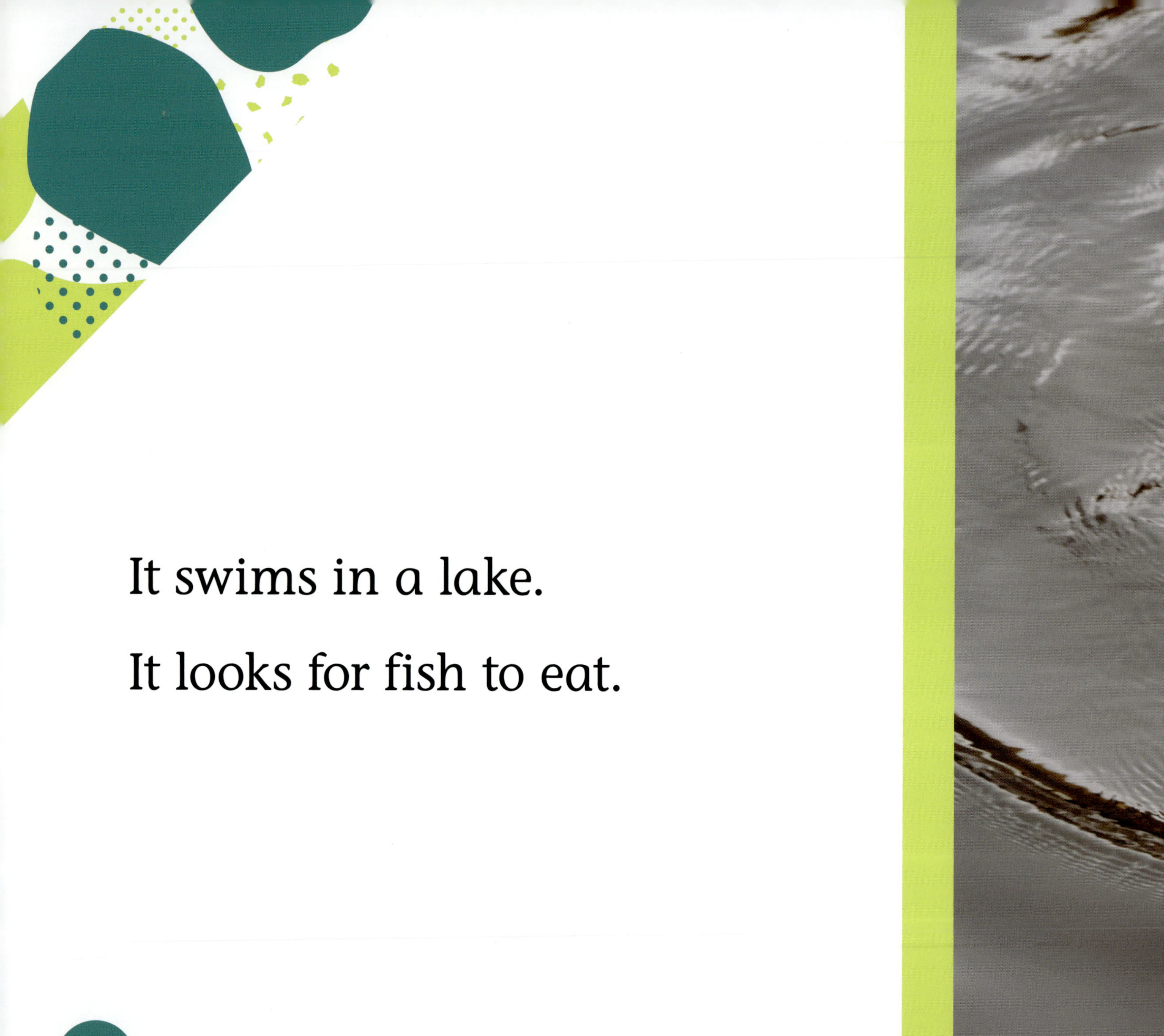

It swims in a lake.

It looks for fish to eat.

It climbs a tree.

It finds some berries.

It sees another raccoon.

They hiss at each other.

The raccoon smells garbage.

It goes through the trash.

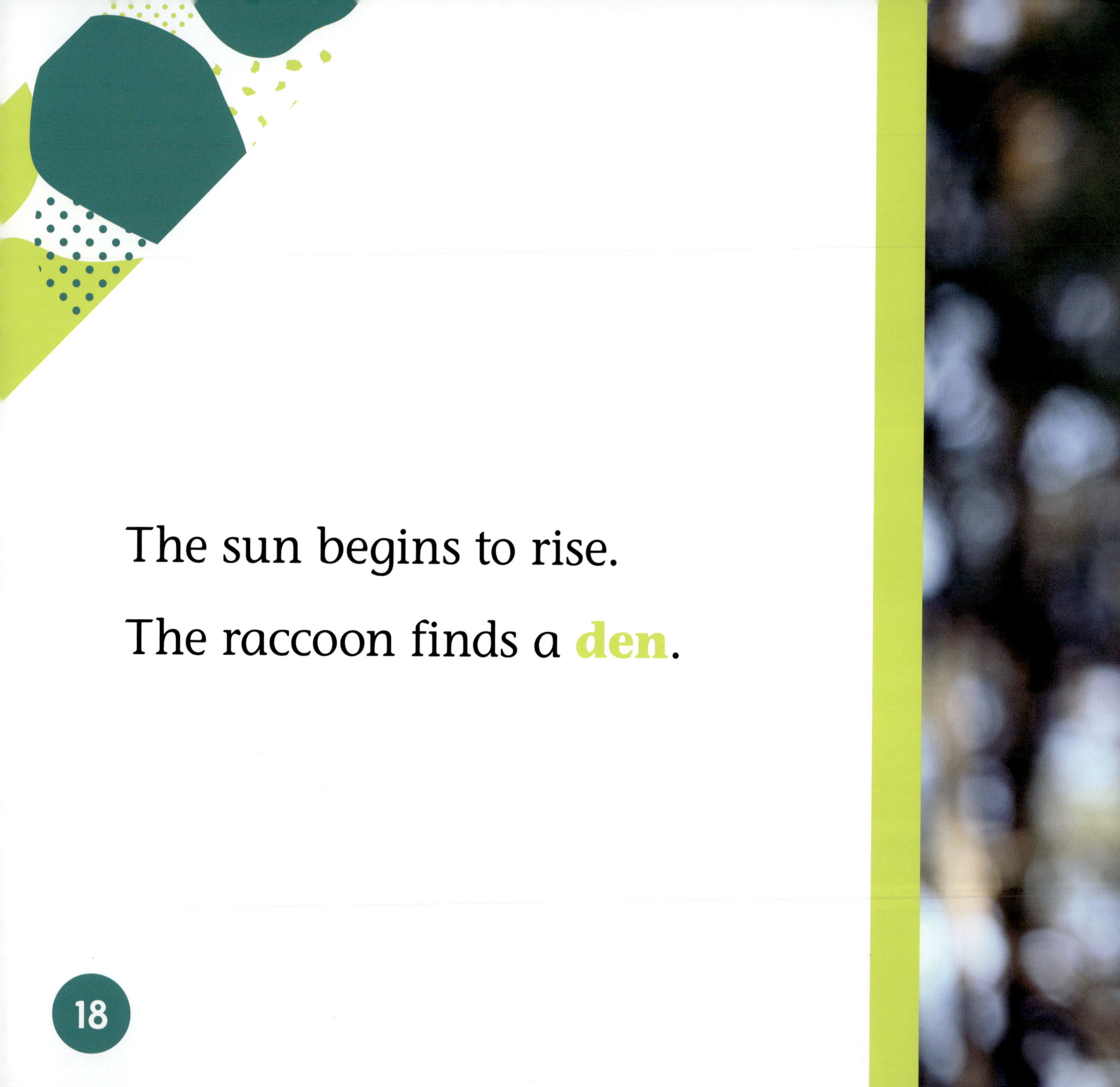

The sun begins to rise.

The raccoon finds a **den**.

It **settles in**.

Time for some rest!

Raccoon Facts

Can live 2 to 3 years in the wild

Usually weighs up to 20 pounds (9.1 kg)

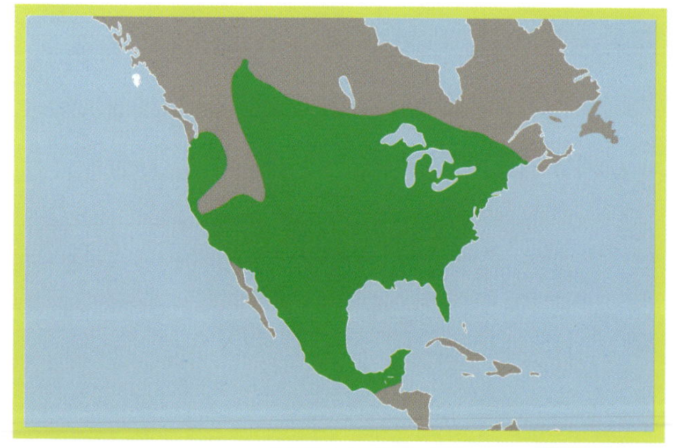

Native to North America

Mother raccoons are very protective of their young

Glossary

den

a resting place for some wild animals.

settle in

to begin to feel comfortable in a new home.

Index

Visit **abdokids.com** to access crafts, games, videos, and more!

Use Abdo Kids code

AAK7312

or scan this QR code!